Money Matters

A Holistic Approach to Building Financial Freedom and Well-Being

Dan Desmarques

22 Lions

Money Matters: A Holistic Approach to Building Financial Freedom and Well-Being

Written by Dan Desmarques

Contents

Introduction

Money Matters: A Holistic Approach to Building Financial Freedom and Well-Being invites you on a profound journey of self-discovery and transformation, where the realms of wealth and spirituality converge to illuminate a path to holistic well-being. In this enlightening exploration, you will unravel the intricate tapestry of beliefs, emotions, and behaviors that shape your relationship with money and success.

Through the lens of ethical wealth management and the cultivation of an abundance mindset, this book delves into the core principles of aligning financial goals with personal values and fostering a deep sense of purpose and integrity in your financial endeavors. Discover the transformative power of mastering your emotions around money as you embark on a journey of self-reflection and empowerment to reprogram your beliefs and attitudes about wealth.

Drawing on the wisdom of behavioral economics and spiritual teachings, this guide offers practical strategies and insights for navigating the complexities of financial decision-making with clarity and mindfulness. Learn to transcend limiting beliefs, embrace a wealth mindset, and make conscious choices that lead to long-term prosperity and fulfillment.

From the importance of exceeding expectations and achieving excellence in all endeavors to the transformative potential of aligning personal values with financial goals, this book provides a roadmap for creating a harmonious relationship with money and abundance. Embrace a holistic approach to financial well-being in which integrity, compassion, and purpose converge to guide you toward a life of prosperity and spiritual growth.

Embark on a journey of self-discovery, empowerment, and transformation as you unlock the secrets of wealth and spirituality. Let this comprehensive guide be your companion as you navigate the intricate dance between money and meaning, leading you to a more fulfilling and prosperous existence.

Chapter 1: The Symbolic Dance of Money

In the realm of human experience, money holds powerful symbolic meaning as a representation of value, wealth, and prosperity. As people navigate the complexities of earning, spending, and managing money, they unwittingly engage in a deeper symbolic dance that reflects their beliefs, values, and attitudes about abundance. At its core, money symbolizes much more than currency or a medium of exchange. It embodies a tangible expression of one's worth, success, and ability to provide for oneself and others. The pursuit of money is often intertwined with the search for self-worth and validation in a society where financial achievement is often equated with personal accomplishment.

Throughout history and across cultures, money has been revered as a powerful symbol of power, status, and influence. Accumulating wealth is seen not only as a means of satisfying material desires, but also as a means of gaining social recognition and establishing one's place in the social hierarchy. Money provides a sense of security and stability, allowing people to control their environment and shape their destiny. But the symbolic nature of money goes beyond its material implications. It serves as a mirror that reflects one's attitudes toward abundance, scarcity, and the flow of resources in one's life.

Those who view money through the lens of scarcity tend to hoard, fear loss, and resist spending, driven by a deep-seated fear of lack. Conversely, those who embrace an abundance mindset see money as a flow of energy that circulates freely to create opportunities for growth, contribution, and fulfillment.

The symbolism of money also extends to notions of worthiness, deservingness, and self-esteem. Many people tie their sense of self-worth to their financial success, believing that their net worth defines their true value as individuals. This conflation of wealth with worthiness can lead to a perpetual cycle of striving, achieving, and never feeling truly fulfilled, as external markers of success fail to fill the void within. In addition, money serves as a symbolic language through which people express their deepest values, priorities, and aspirations.

How people earn, spend, and invest their money reflects their underlying beliefs about what matters most in life-whether it is security, pleasure, status, contribution, or personal growth. By examining their financial habits and choices, we gain insight into their core values and the narratives that drive their actions. We can even assess a person's motivations and level of determinism by evaluating their attitudes toward money. Likewise, we can accurately predict his or her future success simply because we live in a world where success and money are intertwined.

In the grand tapestry of life, money emerges as a multifaceted symbol that weaves together threads of power, security, worth, and self-expression. To decode its symbolic language is to unlock profound insights into one's relationship with abundance, success, and the infinite possibilities that lie beyond the realm of mere currency. A person's spiritual path is determined by his or her relationship with money. Therefore, by embracing a holistic understanding of money as a symbol, we can transcend its material constraints and harness its transformative power to create a life of abundance and deep meaning.

Chapter 2: The Alchemical Journey of Money

Throughout history, money has undergone a fascinating transformation, evolving from a symbolic representation of value to a practical medium of exchange. In ancient times, the concept of money was deeply intertwined with the symbolism of power, wealth, and control. Money was initially perceived as a form of energy essential for acquiring a better life, increasing comfort, and securing basic needs such as health care; in earlier eras, money was symbolized by blood, representing the brutal acquisition of resources by violent means. It was a time when the accumulation of wealth often involved acts of aggression and domination, epitomized by the Vikings and other cultures known for their conquests and riches acquired through barbaric acts.

As societies advanced, money came to symbolize the earth, signifying ownership of land and the rise of tribalism, organizations, and banking systems. This era marked the beginning of the use of agriculture as a means of accumulating wealth and establishing social structures based on land ownership and agricultural productivity. Then, with the advent of the Dark Ages, came the association of money with metals such as gold and silver. During this period, money was perceived as a valuable metal, further solidifying its role as a prominent symbol of wealth and prosperity in various cultures.

Over time, the evolution of money has followed a cyclical pattern that mirrors the elements - water, earth and metal. However, the alchemical chart suggests the absence of the elements of fire and wood, suggesting the impending evolution of the economic system. The current era, represented by wood, signifies a potential shift toward a collapsing economic system due to an overreliance on paper currency derived from wood.

Looking ahead, the narrative of money will enter a new phase with the emergence of digital currencies such as bitcoin and the potential integration of RFID microchips as a form of transaction. This transformation underscores the need to adapt to changing economic landscapes and to understand the intrinsic symbolic value of money beyond its material representation: in essence, the historical evolution of money reveals its profound significance as a symbolic language that reflects societal values, power dynamics, and economic paradigms.

By exploring the symbolic journey of money from blood to metals and beyond, we gain valuable insights into the intricate relationship between wealth, symbolism, and the evolving nature of financial systems. The concept of money as energy delves into the profound understanding that money transcends its material form and serves as a vital force that shapes our lives. Beyond its tangible currency, money embodies a symbolic representation of wealth, value, and prosperity.

Understanding money as energy means recognizing its ability to influence various aspects of our existence, from our material well-being to our emotional and spiritual realms. Because it embodies a form of energy that permeates all aspects of human life, the relationship between money and health underscores the interconnectedness of financial and overall well-being.

Embracing an abundance mindset and understanding the energetic flow of money can lead to greater opportunities for growth, success, and fulfillment. Ultimately, viewing money as energy invites individuals to explore a deeper connection with their financial resources and the symbolic power they hold. By aligning one's beliefs, attitudes, and actions with the energetic essence of money, we can harness its transformative potential to create abundance, prosperity, and a balanced life rooted in purpose and meaning.

Chapter 3: Embracing the Illusory Nature of Money

Understanding the Spiritual Laws of Money explores the intricate relationship between spirituality and financial abundance that transcends conventional notions of wealth. The concept of money as a form of energy intertwined with spiritual principles shapes individual attitudes, beliefs, and actions toward wealth acquisition and prosperity.

One of the fundamental aspects illuminated by the spiritual laws of money is the connection between one's inner value and the outer manifestations of wealth. Money is seen as a reflection of one's soul value, emphasizing the importance of aligning one's actions and intentions with higher spiritual principles in order to attract abundance. By raising consciousness and expanding spiritual awareness, we can tap into the flow of prosperity and create a harmonious balance between material wealth and spiritual growth.

The spiritual nature of money underscores the importance of providing value to others as a path to financial abundance. The law of reciprocity plays a crucial role in wealth creation, emphasizing the importance of giving back to society, supporting charitable causes, and contributing to the well-being of others. By understanding that wealth is a byproduct of providing value and making a positive impact in the world, we can harness the flow of abundance in accordance with universal principles.

In addition, the spiritual laws of money emphasize the role of intention, gratitude, and mindset in attracting prosperity. Cultivating a mindset of abundance and gratitude, while setting clear intentions for financial goals, empowers us to manifest abundance and opportunity in our lives. By aligning thoughts, emotions and actions with positive vibrations of abundance, we can magnetize wealth and unleash the flow of prosperity according to spiritual laws.

The spiritual laws of money also illuminate the relationship between personal growth and financial success. Inner transformation, self-awareness, and spiritual evolution are integral components of wealth manifestation, emphasizing the journey of self-discovery and self-mastery as essential elements in attracting financial abundance. By prioritizing personal development, expanding consciousness, and integrating spiritual practices into daily life, people can elevate their financial reality and cultivate a holistic approach to wealth creation.

In essence, the spiritual laws of money serve as guiding principles that illuminate the sacred connection between spirituality and wealth. By embodying principles of generosity, integrity, and alignment with higher consciousness, we can transcend material limitations and enter a realm of limitless possibility and abundance. The harmonious integration of spiritual values with financial pursuits not only enriches one's material life, but also nourishes the soul, fostering a deeper sense of purpose, fulfillment, and prosperity in alignment with the universal flow of abundance.

Money is essentially a construct based on trust, confidence, and social agreement. The value ascribed to money is not intrinsic, but rather a product of collective beliefs, economic systems, and social constructs. Understanding the illusory nature of money, however, requires a critical examination of its symbolic significance and the role it plays in shaping human experiences and interactions.

The impact of the illusion of money extends beyond the realm of material wealth into complex dynamics of power, status, and self-worth. Society often equates financial success with personal worth, leading individuals to associate their self-esteem and identity with their monetary assets. The illusion of money perpetuates a cycle of materialistic desires, creating a constant pursuit of wealth as a measure of happiness and fulfillment, and intersects with deeper spiritual and philosophical dimensions that reflect the interconnectedness of the material and non-material realms. Thus, while money facilitates economic transactions and material acquisition, its illusory nature challenges individuals to question the true source of abundance and fulfillment.

Disentangling oneself from the illusion of money involves a journey of self-awareness, introspection, and reevaluation of core beliefs about wealth and success, with the illusion of money serving as a gateway to deeper philosophical inquiries into the nature of wealth, value, and human perception. By transcending the material veneer of money and exploring its symbolic essence, individuals can uncover profound truths about the interconnectedness of abundance, spirituality, and personal growth. Embracing a holistic view of money that acknowledges its illusory nature can lead to a mindset shift that fosters a deeper sense of fulfillment, purpose, and resilience in the face of material illusions.

Chapter 4: Balancing Spiritual Growth with Financial Prosperity

The wisdom gleaned from the eternal connection between spirituality and wealth offers profound insights into the human experience. At its core, the relationship between spirituality and wealth is one of symbiosis, not conflict. The narrative that pits spiritual fulfillment against material wealth oversimplifies the dynamic interplay between these forces. Instead, a nuanced perspective reveals that they can complement and enrich each other when approached with mindfulness and wisdom, and that the foundation of this harmony lies in recognizing that wealth and spirituality are not disparate entities, but interconnected strands of the human experience.

The journey to financial success can coexist with spiritual growth when guided by principles of integrity, compassion, and purpose. Striking a balance between the two involves navigating the external world of monetary wealth while nurturing the internal landscape of spiritual well-being. Central to this understanding is the concept that wealth is not inherently antithetical to spirituality.

Rather, it is the intention behind the accumulation of wealth and the manner in which it is used that determines its alignment with spiritual values.

Money, when earned and used mindfully, can be a tool for positive transformation and service to others. But balancing spirituality and wealth is not without challenges. The lure of financial success can sometimes lead individuals astray, causing them to prioritize material gain over spiritual growth. Conversely, a singular focus on spiritual pursuits without financial considerations can hinder one's ability to navigate the practicalities of life in the material world.

Striking a balance between these realms requires a conscious effort to integrate spiritual practices into daily life while approaching financial responsibility from a place of ethical consideration. By adopting a holistic approach that honors both the spiritual and material dimensions of existence, individuals can reap the rewards of prosperity while remaining grounded in spiritual values.

Moreover, the lessons learned from the intersection of spirituality and wealth transcend mere monetary pursuits. They underscore the importance of aligning one's actions with higher principles and fostering an attitude of abundance based on integrity and compassion. By embodying this harmonious relationship, individuals can navigate the complexities of life with grace and purpose.

In essence, the interplay between spirituality and wealth offers a tapestry of lessons that illuminate the path to holistic well-being. It invites us to transcend the dichotomy of materialism versus spirituality and embrace a more integrated and authentic way of living-one that honors both the growth of the soul and the prosperity of the material realm.

In the realm of financial well-being and personal development, the art of money management emerges as a pillar of strength and growth. We must know how to handle our finances with wisdom and foresight for holistic progress. But at the heart of effective money management is the concept of creating money, not just earning it. By creating value and understanding the intrinsic worth of ideas, we can navigate the financial landscape with a fresh perspective.

The notion that selling ideas is the true essence of art, not the art itself, underscores the notion that value and demand intersect to shape prosperous endeavors, and the principle of surrounding oneself with those who are valued and engaging in endeavors that are perceived as valuable underscores the essence of aligning personal values with financial pursuits. Emphasizing the importance of meeting needs rather than imposing will illustrates the subtleties of meeting consumer needs and fostering long-term success in business endeavors.

Basically, we need an abundance of supply, quality, and attention to customer needs to foster satisfaction and drive demand. The anecdote about providing more value than was asked for exemplifies the ethos of exceeding expectations and delivering excellence in all endeavors, whether writing books or running a business.

In addition, exploring the transformative power of mastering the emotions associated with money reveals a self-therapeutic approach to reprogramming beliefs and attitudes about wealth. Through exercises that personify money as a friend and demonstrate love and appreciation for financial abundance, we can shift our mindset toward prosperity and wealth.

Chapter 5: The Interplay of Trust and Wealth

The intricate interplay between money and trust reveals a fundamental relationship that shapes our perceptions and interactions with wealth. Money, as a concept valued by trust, is inextricably linked to the confidence we place in its representation and utility. The perceived value of currency is closely tied to the degree of confidence we have in the stability and reliability of the economic system that underpins it.

The value we place on money is not based solely on its material form, but is deeply rooted in the confidence we have in its ability to function as a medium of exchange, a store of value, and a unit of account. This confidence in the currency we use is essential for the smooth functioning of economic transactions and the overall stability of financial systems.

Confidence also plays a critical role in determining the perceived value of goods and services exchanged for money. When trust between buyers and sellers is high, the perceived value of the products being exchanged is likely to increase, leading to more favorable outcomes for both parties.

Conversely, a lack of trust can undermine the perceived value of transactions, creating uncertainty and hindering economic interactions. But the relationship between trust and wealth goes beyond individual transactions to encompass broader social and cultural dynamics. Social value, much like the perceived value of an individual within a community, is closely tied to the level of trust and respect they command. Building trust with others increases one's social value and opens opportunities for collaboration, growth, and prosperity; and trust serves as a critical component in creating and maintaining personal and professional relationships that can lead to financial success.

Trustworthy interactions foster a sense of security and predictability, enabling a person to engage in economic endeavors with confidence and reliability. In addition, confidence in oneself and one's abilities plays a central role in empowerment and wealth creation. Believing in one's ability to achieve financial goals and make sound decisions is essential to entrepreneurial success and wealth accumulation.

In sum, the intricate relationship between money and trust underscores the profound impact of confidence and reliability on the perceived value of wealth and economic interactions. Trust serves as a cornerstone in shaping our beliefs, behaviors, and relationships with money, influencing not only individual financial outcomes, but also broader societal and cultural perceptions of value and wealth.

As a result, in our modern world, money serves as a mirror that reflects societal values, power dynamics, and patterns of distribution. As individuals assign value to money on a personal and communal level, the concept of currency transcends its physical form to become a symbol of trust, social value, and transactional power.

This connection between trust, value, and money forms the basis for economic transactions and social hierarchies, and a closer look at the social impact of money reveals stark realities about power differentials, economic inequality, and social stratification. Thus, the distribution of wealth within a society reflects not only financial inequalities, but also fundamental inequalities in access to resources, opportunity, and social mobility.

The correlation between wealth and privilege underscores the systemic injustices perpetuated by unequal distribution of wealth, and the role of money in shaping social structures is evident in the areas of employment, education, and quality of life. People often exchange their time and labor for monetary compensation, with implications for well-being, fulfillment, and social status. But the impact of money on education underscores disparities in access to learning opportunities, perpetuating cycles of privilege or disadvantage.

An essential aspect of studying money in society is understanding the relationship between productivity, efficiency, and value creation. Productivity gains driven by economic incentives highlight the intricate balance between individual effort, economic reward, and societal progress. The alignment of individual skills, market demand, and economic value underscores the interconnectedness of wealth creation in a societal context.

Unpacking the social implications of money distribution reveals that wealth is more than a financial asset-it embodies social power, influence, and opportunity. Those in positions of economic privilege often wield significant influence over societal structures, shaping policies, priorities, and resource allocations.

This concentration of wealth and power highlights the need for equitable distribution mechanisms and social policies that promote inclusivity and economic justice. But by critically examining the social impact of money and its distribution patterns, we can strive for a more equitable, inclusive, and responsive economic framework that uplifts communities, fosters empowerment, and promotes sustainable prosperity for all members of society.

Chapter 6: The Path to Sustainable Prosperity

One of the fundamental principles emphasized in the exploration of effective business strategies is the alignment of mind, consciousness and action within the entrepreneurial journey. It is critical to recognize that a holistic approach that encompasses spiritual, psychological, and monetary aspects is essential to maintaining balance and fostering long-term prosperity.

The interconnectedness of these elements underscores the importance of continuous growth and evolution in both the personal and business spheres, and the concept of bankruptcy serves as a sobering reminder of the consequences of imbalance and neglect within the entrepreneurial landscape.

Viewing bankruptcy not only as a financial failure, but as a holistic breakdown that encompasses spiritual, psychological, and monetary facets, prompts introspection into the deeper implications of wealth and success. Understanding that money has meaning beyond its material form, and that strategic alignment with one's purpose and values is essential for sustainable business growth, successful entrepreneurs often transcend the allure of immediate gain and prioritize long-term strategies over short-term pursuits.

A forward-thinking approach that focuses on creating lasting value, nurturing customer relationships, and investing in innovative solutions distinguishes the best entrepreneurs from the rest. The emphasis on strategies over products underscores the value of visionary planning and adaptability in a rapidly evolving business landscape. Such an attitude requires us to trust ourselves and others, in both planning and communication.

This trust shows up in our lives through our self-determination and discipline, because we can't trust ourselves if we can't control our own instincts and accept laziness instead. It shows up when we communicate with others through our ability to reject any form of conversation that nullifies our potential to achieve our results. In fact, before we can find people who will ask us the right questions, we must let go of people who insist on making the most negative judgments, or at least leave them out of our plans.

Later, as we develop our business plan, trust will show up in our communication with consumers. Artists are often poor, not so much because of the inevitability of their own uniqueness, but because of their lack of ability to communicate effectively with others. I once met a writer who complained that he couldn't make much money, and during the conversation he also admitted that he was very rude to his followers. And the question is, how can you expect the people you antagonize to love you for what you do?

Many writers forget that by giving an image of arrogance to people who love their work, that work loses value and interest, and the same goes for anything else. I was successful both as a teacher and as an online retailer because both my students and online shoppers knew they could trust me to respond to their messages and questions and to do exactly what I said I would do. They also knew that they couldn't expect the same from others. The difference was obvious, and so was my rapid popularity as a business owner and teacher.

Trust, a fundamental element of economic transactions, underpins the perceived value of a product and the brand behind it, or even a person and their service, and influences consumer behavior. Understanding the symbiotic relationship between trust and wealth distribution sheds light on the interconnectedness of social structures, economic disparities, and power dynamics within society. These dynamics, however, are often influenced by jealousy.

For example, I didn't have an answer for my colleagues who asked why certain universities asked me to teach subjects that they were qualified to teach and I wasn't, because they expected to get the extra income based on their skills, and instead people would choose me based on the trust they had in my work, and this because skills and results are not necessarily related.

One person may have the skills and knowledge that led to their acquisition and be incompetent at producing results, while another person may have acquired the skills and knowledge on their own and produce effective results. A college degree alone does not guarantee results. In fact, most of the jobs I have had in my life had nothing to do with what I learned through others, but what I learned on my own. People were confident in the results they were getting because they could see that others weren't getting results despite their qualifications.

One of the most common things I see in people is that they are selfish, both in their jobs, the services they provide and the businesses they want to develop, and this is the cause of their downfall. They lack social value, spiritual awareness and the ability to see the multidimensional nature of entrepreneurial endeavors. They are unable to transcend the need for immediate profit and embrace long-term sustainability. As a result, they face challenges they can't overcome, are unable to increase productivity and profitability, and end up postponing their most urgent tasks.

Many of them also fail to transcend conventional business paradigms by challenging traditional notions of success and prosperity, so they almost invariably try to succeed along well-trodden paths that don't add much value. They lack the discernment and emotional intelligence to evaluate their decisions and the courage to venture into the unknown. If they had more faith in themselves and were able to align with broader societal values, nurture customer relationships, and address core organizational deficiencies, they would more easily navigate the complexities of the modern entrepreneurial landscape and chart a path to lasting prosperity, strategic resilience, and societal impact.

Chapter 7: Transforming Poverty into Wealth

Examining the ethical implications of financial matters illuminates the moral complexities inherent in the pursuit and management of money. At the heart of ethical reflection is the recognition that our unconscious beliefs play a significant role in shaping our attitudes and behaviors toward money.

The realization that more than 80% of our actions stem from deep-seated beliefs underscores the importance of introspection and conscious awareness in navigating financial decisions. It also means that if you are not aware of your daily need to reframe your beliefs, you are most likely to fail at anything that requires a change in thought patterns and a paradigm shift in your reality.

In other words, you must believe that you can be rich before you can actually be rich, and this requires that you visualize and feel rich before you can have it. You should be more comfortable with wealth than you are with poverty. And while this may sound simple, since no one wants to be poor, the truth is that most people are uncomfortable with wealth, which is why they spend it as fast as they earn it.

Acquiring a wealth mindset requires that you learn to save your money and appreciate having it. It also requires that you associate your emotions with wealth by enjoying things that wealthy people do, such as traveling, eating well, and acquiring a more uplifting view of life. This may sound difficult, or like you need money to make more money, and while it is partially true that the more you have, the more you can get, there are other ways to exercise your mind with these recommendations.

For example, you may not know famous and wealthy people, but you can read what they write, their memories, and adopt their habits of mind. The 38 Letters of J.D. Rockefeller to His Son are a good example of this, because while he was sharing information about wealth and social values, you can access and learn from these letters as if you were the son of the richest man in the world.

There are many other examples of people sharing their thoughts and beliefs in books that you can read. The more you do this, the more you will learn from people you have never met and who may even be dead. In the end, you will be changed by the information you gain.

When I read a lot, people perceived me as a strange young person because I had formulated conclusions that did not correspond to my reality. I was poor, I looked poor, and I had never traveled anywhere in the world. But I had already accumulated a great wealth of knowledge, and even though this knowledge seemed to contradict my reality, it would later contribute to my potential to change it.

Without the abundance of books I read on the Law of Attraction, I probably would not have changed my brain to the point of creating a new world for myself, moving between parallel realities, and instead would still be struggling to survive, going through the exact same challenges. But most people are so stuck in the same struggles that they learn to call them normal and then accept them, dying exactly as they have always lived, in absolute misery and suffering.

Anything beyond the reality they know is an impossibility, a lie, which is why these same people accuse me of being a drug dealer or doing something else illegal. Because they are too stupid to change, they must perceive those who do not as wiser, but as criminals. In fact, that's how the stupid perceive reality, as a world where you have to do something illegal to change it, because they are incapable of changing anything about themselves. And what misery it is when you accept that you are who you are and not a product of your own creation.

So the most painful karma you can give your enemies is not to fight them and not to give them any information. I learned the meaning of turning the other cheek, as Yeshua recommended from the Scriptures, when I saw over many decades that people refuse to change and instead try to stop you when you want to change, and insult and slander you when you do change. So the worst thing you can do for them is not to hate them, but to leave them in their own ignorance, for such ignorance perpetuates their reality.

Nowadays when the same people talk to me, it's like I'm going back in time because the person they're talking to doesn't exist anymore, but they don't know, they're still stuck in the same reality where nothing has ever changed. They can't perceive my changes because that would mean perceiving the stagnation in themselves, and as a result the real me is invisible to them. They make me feel like a ghost because they are not really talking to me but to their imaginary version of who I am.

It is also not difficult to enjoy things that rich people do when you realize that some of the poorest places on earth are also some of the most visited by tourists. Just look around you and notice the value of the things you have not appreciated. This appreciative mindset will lead you to the rich mindset you are trying to create.

For example, when I was poor, I used to visit the wealthier areas of my city and look at the streets, the houses, and feel the emotions in the air that were fueled by the energies of the residents. I did not judge the way they stared at me, but focused on the things that were free, like a walk on the beach, or cheap, like an espresso in a coffee shop where I was welcomed with a smile.

These experiences helped me shift my attention from poverty to wealth, so that even though I lived in apartments where I was ashamed to invite friends, I could experience a wealthy mindset during the day just by being in areas where I could feel wealthy. The ability to separate my emotional state from my financial state helped me gain the mental space to follow the path that led me to where I am now. And I eventually forgot that immense suffering, although I am reminded of it whenever I return to Europe, because

I transformed it into resilience and self-discipline. Now I am not afraid of being poor because I know how to be rich and I love the life I have.

Chapter 8: Integrating Ethics into Financial Matters

The interplay of power, money, and upbringing underscores the influence of early exposure to wealth and privilege in shaping individuals' attitudes toward money. Of course, those who are surrounded by wealth from an early age are often guided toward a mindset of abundance and responsible financial stewardship, while individuals raised in less affluent environments may struggle with a mindset of scarcity and ingrained beliefs about the value of money.

Religions, in particular, often play a negative role in people's minds by associating virtue with suffering and wealth with deception and evil. As a result, guilt acts as a corrosive force that undermines personal responsibility and demotivates us from pursuing our dreams. We feel guilty for wanting more because we are told that love is found among people who want less for us and will resent our achievements, especially when we get much more than they expected of us.

Recognizing the detrimental effects of guilt on one's relationship with money and others underscores the importance of fostering a sense of responsibility for our own existence rather than allowing others to dictate our outcomes. After all, if we are the only ones dealing with the consequences, why should we allow others to dictate the experience?

Taking responsibility for our financial success also means that we may have to neglect the value of the people who oppress us. Our love for others and our altruism toward humanity should not include naivety and acceptance of those who not only don't understand these qualities, but despise them and see them as weaknesses.

Certainly, I quickly lose interest in sharing what I know with those who do not do the same and instead see me as a fool for being compassionate while they see others as competition. Our conversations are motivated by different interests, and my virtues are perceived by them as flaws.

Also, whenever you share what you know with jealous people, you are more likely to face opposition through lies, sabotage of your efforts, and slander. Only those who see life as a collaboration and exchange of ideas can uphold holistic values and accept you as you are, with both weaknesses and strengths, and see the real weaknesses and strengths in you, while the jealous people you meet along the way do the exact opposite and make you mistake your strengths for weaknesses and weaknesses for strengths.

The people who tried to stop me from becoming a successful writer would find mistakes in my writing or tell me I didn't look like a writer, and neither situation determines my worth, though they do cause many who seek the same result to question themselves. None of them ever noticed that my background as a teacher and business manager or the thousands of books I read on finance, manifestation, and spirituality would help me succeed because none of them were interested in seeing me succeed. They were betting on my failure.

People have to be right, and when I failed, I proved them right. When I succeeded, I proved them wrong and showed them that they are insignificant compared to me, and they hate that, and that is why I lost all the friendships I had. However, the same thing happens with my readers who confuse sharing knowledge with arrogance and then insult me in their book reviews by saying that I am a narcissist. Why would I be a narcissist when I am sharing everything I know to help you succeed and get more out of life faster than I ever did?

I am literally condensing years of my life into a few pages so you can get more in less time. But am I arrogant, narcissistic, and evil for doing this? These people are selfish. They write these things because they don't want other people to read the books. My writing makes them feel insignificant, and they know that if others read these books, the success of those readers will make them feel even worse, so they do their best to make sure that fewer people find the books and read them. And what a shame of the world we live in when the majority believes what the majority says, because if you don't read a book because of what someone else said about it, you're less likely to find the lessons you need.

The most popular books don't threaten anyone's status quo, and that's why they get promoted. They are nothing more than common sense books that in many cases teach you to accept life as it is and do nothing about it. In fact, much of the hostility toward the rich comes from a great financial inequality. The poorer people are, the more likely they are to hate powerful books on how to acquire wealth. They hate the book because they can't accept it, they hate it because they can't change, and they hate it because they know others will read it and change.

This is envy, resentment, and a projection of self-hatred, all at once, directed at the author of such writings. And how can someone be so full of hate to the point of manifesting insanity when they reject the very things they envy?

We cannot challenge social norms that equate wealth with negative connotations by accepting them, or change our destiny by hating those who have what we want. By reframing perspectives on wealth distribution and acknowledging the interconnectedness of wealth and social structures, we can cultivate a more nuanced understanding of ethical considerations in financial matters. Central to the ethical discourse surrounding money is the recognition that financial success is intertwined with spiritual and psychological maturity.

Understanding that wealth enhances one's inherent qualities underscores the importance of aligning financial aspirations with personal values and fulfillment. We grow as people and as souls when we understand that our relationship with money is at the core of our relationship with the world and with life itself, and affects not only how we live, but how everyone lives. We need more introspection, social awareness, and moral discernment before we can see how our relationship with money is directly related to how we want to live our lives and what kind of world we want to live in.

In other words, if you don't like your boss, stop working for him; if you don't believe in the positive impact your company has on the world, leave; if you want to be rich, choose something you believe in and then do your best at it, not just because you want to be rich, but because you know the world is a better place with people like you. Incorporating ethical considerations into financial matters not only promotes personal growth and well-being, but also contributes to a more ethical and harmonious society.

Chapter 9: The Alchemy of Money and Emotions

Exploring the intricate relationship between money and emotions reveals a profound connection that shapes our mental and psychological well-being. The influence of money on emotional states serves as a key determinant in understanding the dynamics of wealth, happiness, and spiritual fulfillment.

Beyond its material significance, money carries a symbolic weight that is intertwined with our emotional landscape. People often attach deep-seated emotions such as fear, anxiety, happiness, and satisfaction to financial matters that reflect their values, beliefs, and experiences. Understanding this emotional currency is paramount to navigating the complexities of wealth and its impact on personal fulfillment.

The interplay between money and emotions transcends mere financial transactions and penetrates the core of human consciousness. Emotions such as resentment, joy, anger, and fear are intricately woven into our perceptions of wealth and abundance, and the emotional frequencies we emit, whether positive or negative, significantly influence our financial outcomes and life experiences.

There is a correlation between emotional frequencies and financial success. Individuals operating from higher emotional frequencies characterized by trust, positivity, and gratitude tend to attract wealth effortlessly, while lower emotional frequencies characterized by self-pity, resentment, and fear often lead to financial struggles and setbacks.

We must cultivate a positive emotional relationship with money in order to manifest abundance and financial well-being. Embracing trust, faith, and hard work as guiding principles paves the way for a harmonious alignment with wealth and success. Shifting from negative emotions to a mindset of abundance and gratitude sets the stage for transformative changes in one's financial reality.

By identifying and addressing deep-seated emotional barriers, we can embark on a journey of self-discovery and financial empowerment. Reprogramming emotional patterns and beliefs around money through self-therapeutic exercises and positive affirmations becomes a catalyst for attracting wealth and prosperity. Repeating these affirmations every day can actually help you align your mind with a more positive outlook on the prospect of becoming wealthy. All you need to do to create such an affirmation is to attach a positive emotion to it.

This exercise is even more powerful if you associate familiar states of mind with the same emotions. For example, you can say: I love eating, but I love being rich and eating in the best restaurants even more. Or you can say: I love seeing my partner smile, and I love even more the fact that I can buy them expensive gifts that they love. Or you might say instead: I love my job because it helps me make more money, and with that money I can travel, make new friends, and explore all that life has to offer.

As you can see, it's pretty impossible to hate money when you associate it with the things you value, which is why reminding yourself of this connection every day through positive affirmations can actually shift your mind from a state of lack to one of abundance. You will notice this when your mind becomes very creative in saving money and coming up with ideas to make more.

This happens to me all the time. When my partner asks me for a pizza, I immediately compare the best places to eat with their prices and see that quality and cost are not correlated, which means I can eat well for less. And if I want to write a good book, I look at the questions my readers ask me, because they certainly have not found the answers in the content of my previous writings.

For the average person, this constant thinking and analyzing may sound exhausting, but only because they have negative emotions associated with money. They don't want to think about it, even though they use it every day. And by distancing themselves from something they use every day, they actually attract more scarcity.

The solution is more the opposite, it is to look at your wealth as a game. Just ask yourself: How much more money can I put in my bank account this month? What could I do in my spare time that would help me get more money?

You don't have to worry about going from pennies to pounds in a short period of time if you focus on changing your mindset about money. Just focus on the satisfaction of earning an extra dollar that should only come from your work. For example, could you bake some cookies and sell them online? Could you make some natural soap and sell it on social media? What could you do that would be pleasurable, therapeutic, fun, and help you make more money?

In essence, exploring money and emotions illuminates the profound connection between internal states and external manifestations of wealth. By recognizing the impact of emotions on financial outcomes, you can embark on a path of self-mastery, abundance, and holistic well-being while developing a positive but transformative relationship with money that leads to emotional fulfillment.

Chapter 10: Money as a Symbol of Trust and Prosperity

The study of money as both a unit of account and a means of payment underscores its dual function in economic systems. As a unit of account, money facilitates the measurement and comparison of the value of different economic goods and services, providing a common measure for valuing transactions and assets. As a means of payment, money facilitates the exchange of goods and services, thereby promoting economic activity and enabling the flow of resources within a society.

The interplay between money, productivity and social welfare reflects a dynamic relationship that goes beyond mere monetary transactions. Productivity and efficiency are intrinsic factors that influence the creation and circulation of wealth, highlighting the critical role of human effort and innovation in shaping the value of money. By recognizing the interconnectedness of economic activities and personal contributions, we can appreciate the nuanced dynamics that underpin monetary value, and examining money in relation to cultural perceptions and societal norms sheds light on the diverse interpretations and implications of wealth.

Cultural beliefs, historical contexts, and social structures help shape individuals' attitudes toward money and influence notions of success, wealth, and status; thus, the true value of money transcends its material form and encapsulates a myriad of meanings, beliefs, and socioeconomic dynamics.

By recognizing money as a symbol of trust, a medium of exchange, and a reflection of societal values, we can develop a deeper appreciation for the multifaceted role of currency in shaping personal, social, and economic spheres. Money serves as a medium through which individuals express their desires, intentions, and attitudes toward wealth accumulation. By fostering a harmonious relationship with money and embracing an abundance mindset, we can cultivate a sense of prosperity that transcends mere monetary wealth and helps to attract more of it.

Self-awareness, emotional intelligence, and gratitude are the foundation of our ability to shape our financial journey. Understanding the role of emotions in magnetizing wealth and opportunity highlights the power of positive thinking, visualization, and intention setting in attracting financial abundance; therefore, by cultivating a mindset of abundance and gratitude, we can tap into the universal flow of prosperity and manifest our financial goals with clarity and purpose.

This pursuit of personal wealth requires a holistic approach that integrates financial success with principles of integrity, compassion, and social responsibility. By aligning financial pursuits with ethical values and spiritual principles, we can create a foundation for lasting prosperity that extends beyond financial gain to personal growth and societal impact.

Personal prosperity is then measured not only by monetary wealth, but also by a holistic sense of well-being that includes physical health, emotional balance, and meaningful relationships. The link between money and personal fulfillment underscores the importance of aligning financial goals with broader life goals and values. By integrating wealth creation with personal growth, we can embark on a journey of prosperity that enriches not only our bank accounts, but also the overall quality of life for ourselves and others.

There are numerous examples of individuals and countries that have used their rise from humble beginnings to achieve great success with altruistic motives or ideas that benefit humanity. One such individual is Howard Schultz, the former CEO of Starbucks. Growing up in a poor housing project in Brooklyn, Schultz worked hard to overcome his circumstances and eventually revolutionized the coffee industry by creating a company that prioritized social responsibility and employee well-being. Starbucks became known for providing health benefits and stock options to its employees, pioneering a new model of corporate social responsibility.On a national level, Bhutan is a country that has adopted a unique economic model that focuses on promoting Gross National Happiness (GNH) rather than Gross Domestic Product (GDP). By prioritizing the well-being of its citizens and environmental protection over material wealth, Bhutan has set an example for sustainable development and holistic prosperity. The country's commitment to environmental sustainability, cultural preservation, and equitable development has inspired global conversations about alternative economic paradigms that prioritize human flourishing over mere economic growth.

Another example is the case of Costa Rica, a country that has prioritized environmental conservation and sustainable development to drive economic growth. By focusing on ecotourism, renewable energy, and biodiversity conservation, Costa Rica improved its economic prospects while benefiting the planet and its people. This approach not only boosted the country's economy, but also served as a model for sustainable development practices that other nations could adopt to achieve both financial prosperity and environmental stewardship.

These examples demonstrate how individuals and countries can go from rags to riches by embracing altruistic ideas or strategies that make a positive contribution to society and the world at large. By aligning financial pursuits with ethical values, social responsibility, and a vision for the greater good, it is possible to achieve prosperity that transcends monetary wealth and creates a lasting impact on individuals, communities, and the planet.

Chapter 11: The Future of Money

The evolution of financial systems and the emergence of new technologies will revolutionize the dynamics of wealth accumulation and monetary transactions, ushering in an era of unprecedented change and innovation.

A central theme that resonates in discussions about the future of money is the impending transition to a more diversified and inclusive monetary ecosystem. The traditional reliance on paper money will give way to a broader range of options, driven by the need for greater market flexibility and global financial integration.

The dawn of a new era requires a global currency that transcends borders, uniting diverse economies and paving the way for equal economic opportunity across regions. This evolution toward a global currency is underpinned by a critical shift toward recognizing the value of real estate as a cornerstone of financial stability and prosperity. Real estate, more than traditional assets such as gold, is expected to play a pivotal role in shaping future wealth creation and sustainability.

The re-emphasis on real estate ownership represents a return to core principles that underscore the importance of tangible assets in driving economic growth and investment resilience, and the future landscape of money is seen as inextricably linked to advances in renewable energy and innovative technologies. The rise of sustainable energy solutions and transformative inventions will redefine the way we perceive and use financial resources, moving from a society dependent on the centralization of energy resources manipulated by a few corporations to one that is independent and self-sufficient.

We are already seeing a glimpse of this transition with concepts such as the conversion of solar energy into usable power and the need for alternative but environmentally friendly ways to fuel our vehicles. Soon the entire world will run on resources that are independent of any financial monopoly. That is, of course, if we can move from a world dominated by greed to one of altruism and greater awareness of our resources and interdependence as a planetary collective species, divided not by borders but only by ideals.

Of course, along the way, certain regulations must fall into disuse, such as the need for passports, borders, and control over our movements on the planet. We see glimpses of this in the European Union. And hopefully this ideal, along with the special visas created specifically for nomads who want to work abroad, will give rise to a new planetary collective.

If you want to position yourself ahead of others, you have to move towards that future in mind and spirit. It is the awareness that the world needs an ascension to more love and cooperation that will lead you to your ideal future. Surely whatever you decide to do to become more abundant will succeed if you align it with a triangulation of an idealization of a better Earth, your need to contribute to humanity with your purpose, and the benefits that more abundance will bring you along the way.

You are more likely to attract abundance when you align it with your honest intentions, which is why whenever someone asks me for help in finding their ideal life purpose, especially one that can make them very wealthy, my answer is always the same: Look around you and find opportunities to expand human consciousness. There are so many ways to do this that once you shift your consciousness from needing for yourself to giving to others, you will find an abundance of opportunities. This is what it means to have an abundance mindset.

Wherever I go, I find such opportunities and then I share them with the locals, and those who listen and apply what I say become wealthy in a short time, while the rest continue to struggle with their lack of faith, laziness and preconceived notions about the world. People always fail more because of their doubts than because of the ideas they implement. By gambling on their own security and what they know, most people invest in their failure, because the future wants nothing of the past. If you want to get rich, you must always invest in the future.

One of the most obvious ways to perceive opportunities is through the establishments we see everywhere, namely coffee shops that sell exactly the same things. What an advantage those who sell unique things have over those who dare not even copy their ideas. But what is even more interesting is that the places that sell new pastries are not even inventing anything new, but simply importing the unknown and making it visible to locals who might otherwise never have seen it. I am talking about bakeries in China, Malaysia, and the Philippines that are increasing their profits and popularity by selling bread and cakes from Greece, France, Spain, Italy, and Portugal.

If we look at real estate, it is also very obvious that modern designs that copy the best ideas from around the world sell faster than old and outdated designs. We see the same tendency in art, with painters who embrace the need for innovation outselling their peers who still use traditional methods. We may call it modern art, but it is much more than ideas, it is the stimulation of the intellect in an oversaturated world of information and chaos that puts the best artists at the forefront of innovation and attention, and they gather all the wealth while the rest struggle to sell, claiming that art is unappreciated.

When it comes to books, and as the owner of a book publishing company, these principles couldn't be more obvious to me, because I'm constantly encountering authors or people who want to publish a book with absolutely nothing useful to say. They want their name on an important product to feel validated, and yet they don't care if their words are nothing more than a reinvention of what others have said, or simply a need to soothe their ego by talking to themselves. Their words have no intrinsic value, and how can a writer be unique and contribute to the world with such a vast array of options?

As someone who has hit the bestseller lists more than 100 times under multiple pen names, I can give you a clear answer: By writing something that people need and cannot find anywhere else. And the way to write something of quality that can't be found anywhere else is the same for any successful endeavor: Read a lot, find untapped information between the lines and behind the thoughts of authors, explore that information through your own life and the lives of those you encounter, and focus on making a contribution to society.

Instead of looking at the prospect of simply selling dreams and emotions, consider how the lives of others will be shaped by your words. If you can do that, you can write a very good book. However, most people get so caught up in the need to be perceived as an author that they end up focusing almost entirely on sentence structure, writing eloquently but without valuable meanings, and I personally don't care how good a book is if it has nothing to teach me, because value always trumps quality of words.

We see this principle in business too, because while many entrepreneurs obsess over the quality of their product, the successful ones simply look at how people respond to it. Just as a book that no one reads is a worthless book, a product that no one buys is a useless product, no matter how much time you put into promoting it. This is why so many college graduates fail as entrepreneurs, they get too caught up in the theories to look at the results. They spend too much time on the processes and waste too much time thinking about nothing but useless thoughts.

Chapter 12: The Intersection of Consciousness and Wealth

Whenever someone wants to do business with me, but takes too long to do what they say and promise, I already know that they are just wasting my time and looking for a reinforcement to solve their procrastination, but with no long-term impact on their resolve. Most people just don't have what it takes to have a wealth mindset, no matter how much they read about it. And the solution for them is even more ignored than the right qualities - it means developing discipline and analyzing the source of their ignorance by questioning themselves.

The rapidly growing need for coaches is nothing more than a business opportunity to replace the uselessness of certified therapists, because a psychologist or psychiatrist who wastes your time and can't help you achieve your goals, and instead obsesses over your childhood and drugs you, can't really help you go anywhere but out the door of your apartment and into his office every week, or keep your job, just enough to keep his business going.

You also don't need certification to produce results for yourself and others while contributing to a better world. Often you don't even need the products. One of my students developed a business with nothing more than an idea I gave her. Years later, she hired classmates to work for her, and what she was doing was nothing more than applying what she was already doing as an interpreter. The only difference is that instead of waiting for clients to arrive in the country and send her a message, she created business investment packages that she would offer to companies in South America. Her packages included everything someone looking to invest in a Chinese factory would want - knowledge of potential manufacturers, a translator and interpreter to accompany the group on a daily basis, hotel bookings, restaurant bookings, and so on. Once they paid her, they had nothing else to worry about.

She became so wealthy that her classmates, out of curiosity, asked me what I had told her. The answer was not what they expected: I told her what I told everyone else because I shared it in the classroom. Many were playing with their cell phones while I was speaking because they didn't think what I was talking about was important and related to their exams, others were complaining to my colleagues that I was wasting their time teaching unrelated topics, and only this girl was copying and applying the information I was sharing. When these students asked me to repeat what I had told them that day, I said: Read my books, because I am no longer your teacher.

Many times people miss the best opportunities of their lives simply because they are not paying attention. Many other of my students from other universities applied the ideas I shared with them and became extremely wealthy and happy with their lives. They were not even the best students and the ideas were not extraordinary. I simply shared with them what I observed in their country and combined their abilities with obvious needs that could benefit many. This is the formula for success, but because people are too obsessed with money to care about the needs of others, they fail to look, and looking is the most important skill of a good entrepreneur.

Another problem many people have besides not looking is not seeing, like when they think their teacher is an idiot because he is supposed to teach something from a book and knows nothing about economics. But even worse, they don't listen, because the reason I was often asked to teach their teachers how to teach, and even give classes on how to write a resume and how to act in an interview, is because I had worked as a business manager before working for universities. They also ignored this obvious fact.

People are blind, deaf and too stupid to see the opportunities in front of them and then claim that they are unlucky, but just as luck favors the prepared mind, those who are too stupid always feel that luck is not on their side. If you work hard with what someone shares with you and become successful beyond belief, the same lazy, uneducated, and closed-minded people will tell you that you are very lucky. That's how useless their opinions are, even as they complain about those who try to help them, simply because such help does not conform to their prejudices and assumptions about the reality they wish to perpetuate.

Those who put the most effort into keeping the world as it is, instead of moving it toward a better future, are always more likely to fail in life, and for obvious reasons - they are investing in the past. Their minds are asleep, there is no creativity, emotion or motivation in them for the prospect of creating a better world for others or themselves, they can only envy and covet what others have. But the more one focuses on opportunities that are aligned with higher consciousness, the more likely one is to succeed. This is why spiritual principles are always aligned with prosperity.

This doesn't mean that you should confuse religion with spirituality, because they are not the same, and religion is nothing more than a set of agreed-upon principles about spirituality and human nature that often lead people to a belief rather than a reality. There is nothing of God in the imposition of beliefs and dogmas. They are demon-worshipping arenas. There is more God in a heavy metal concert than in a church, because the real God is the God of creativity, emotional expression, self-awareness, and questioning.

If you want to know God, you must first learn to question and study His answers. Then you will see that God answers your prayers every day with everything that comes to you. Even your deceased loved ones are helping you from the spirit world by setting the stage for the miracles that will come your way. All you have to do is accept these gifts and understand their meaning. In fact, many times they have simply cooperated in bringing the right people into your life.

One of these great gifts is a supportive partner, and all you have to do is respect and appreciate him or her and flow with that energy into a better existence. So many men have become greater, not because of what they learned or did, but because of the women who came into their lives with love, courage and faith. But what a miserable world it is when women are told they're better off alone, because that's a world where promiscuity, dementia, loneliness and misery spread. When women don't understand their role as nurturers and men lose interest in building healthy families, society cannot sustain itself and is driven to its downfall by depression and suicide, as well as a total lack of moral values and ambition.

Chapter 13: The Power of Subconscious Beliefs in Financial Wealth Creation

As the financial world continues to evolve, the interplay between digital currencies and traditional monetary systems will shape the future of wealth management and transactions. The emergence of digital coins represents a paradigm shift toward decentralized and secure financial mechanisms. The integration of cutting-edge technologies such as RFID microchips underscores the potential for revolutionary changes in how we perceive, transact, and store wealth in the digital age.

The problem we may face is not so much the technologies themselves, but the attempt by a few to use them to control the masses and redirect this potential future to themselves, limiting the possibilities for true entrepreneurship. The future of money ushers in a new era of financial consciousness where values of sustainability, innovation and inclusiveness converge to redefine the dynamics of wealth creation and distribution, but we must be aware of the attempt by some to monopolize such a future as they have done with our past and the technologies that have been developed.

For example, the light bulb is an invention that is not so great compared to the model proposed by Nikola Tesla, which could revolutionize the world and advance it by many thousands of years. When we look at the state of technology we have and compare it to the vast amount of suppressed knowledge, it is inevitable to realize that we are many thousands of years behind the world we should have, and this need to correct our path will not happen until we ascend in consciousness and realize the deceptions that continue to this day.

It is necessary to stop those who are motivated by greed and support those who are motivated by altruistic values of global cooperation and equalization of benefits and opportunities for the people of the planet. Much of this process will require us to look at what has been suppressed or neglected and forgotten, rather than at new ideas or inventions. Harnessing the transformative potential of technology, sustainability and global connectivity is key to unlocking a future where prosperity is not just an aspiration, but a shared reality for individuals and societies around the world.

In this potential landscape, the future of money is as real as what we can do for others, because it will evolve as we evolve as a planetary species. We are moving there because we already understand that books have value in their own right, even in digital form. Hopefully, as more people are willing to pay for knowledge and information, and as this process becomes more accessible to the masses, the possibility of a better Earth will become a reality within our reach.

On the other hand, not much can be done for an ignorant people, because ignorant people can't see or appreciate good things. That's what ignorance is, the inability to see value, so ignorance leads to failure, and failure leads to misery. If you want to get rich, you have to educate yourself first, and that starts with books. I have never met anyone who failed because he did not have a college degree, but I have never met a successful entrepreneur who did not read a lot.

Exploring the unknown through reading and learning reveals the hidden influences that shape our perceptions of wealth and prosperity, sheds light on the profound impact of our beliefs on financial success and well-being, and expands our potential to manifest our dreams. Will alone is never enough; you must learn, change, and improve. And while failure does not determine your results, you are unlikely to succeed unless you are willing to learn from those failures and improve.

The subconscious beliefs and mindsets we hold play a pivotal role in shaping our financial reality. The deep-seated beliefs we hold about money, wealth and success, often based on the paradigms of the people around us, form the basis of our financial decisions and behaviors. Much of what leads us to failure is rooted in the false paradigms, fears and beliefs of others. These beliefs, often ingrained in us from childhood or through societal conditioning, dictate our relationship with wealth and influence our financial decisions in subtle but significant ways.

Understanding the power of beliefs in the financial realm is essential to unlocking our true wealth potential. The subconscious mind acts as a silent orchestrator, shaping our financial trajectory based on the beliefs and thought patterns we hold. By delving into our subconscious beliefs about money, we can unravel the hidden barriers and limiting beliefs that may be hindering our financial growth and abundance. It is in our subconscious mind that we can unravel the intricate web of beliefs that underpin our financial decisions and behaviors.

We do this by questioning our own thoughts and decisions and rationalizing ways to improve them through thought and systemic discipline. Without self-discipline, nothing changes. But it all begins with a schedule and commitment to our goals within a self-imposed transaction of time and results. By uncovering the hidden belief systems that drive our financial decisions, we can consciously reprogram our minds for success and prosperity. This process involves challenging and reframing limiting beliefs, cultivating a mindset of abundance, and aligning our thoughts and actions with our financial goals.

By cultivating a deeper understanding of our subconscious beliefs and their influence on financial outcomes, we can embark on a path of conscious wealth creation and fulfillment. Start by writing down on a piece of paper everything your parents said or taught you about money, and you will begin to understand which subconscious beliefs are holding you back.

This introspective exploration allows you to harness the power of your beliefs to manifest financial abundance and prosperity in alignment with your true desires and aspirations, because it reveals a profound connection between your subconscious mindset and financial reality. By delving into the depths of your beliefs about wealth, abundance and success, you can unlock the hidden potential for financial growth and prosperity.

Chapter 14: The Intersection of Perception and Wealth in Financial Success

The essence of integrating discipline and strategy into money matters lies in the ability to anticipate potential challenges, capitalize on opportunities, and effectively navigate the complex landscape of financial growth.

A key aspect of applying strategy to financial endeavors is the emphasis on setting clear and achievable goals. By defining specific financial objectives and outlining a roadmap to achieve them, we can chart a course for success. Strategic goal setting provides direction and a sense of purpose in managing finances, enabling individuals to stay focused and committed to their financial goals.

In addition, strategic financial planning involves assessing risks and opportunities, analyzing market trends, and making informed investment decisions. Through thorough research, we can identify potential areas for growth, mitigate risk, and take advantage of market opportunities. Strategic investment decisions based on sound research and analysis can lead to sustainable wealth creation and financial stability over time.

Incorporating contingency planning into financial strategies is essential to mitigate unforeseen circumstances and ensure long-term financial security. Establishing emergency funds, insurance coverage and diversified investment portfolios are strategic measures to protect against unexpected setbacks and financial downturns. In addition, strategic planning includes ongoing monitoring and evaluation of financial performance to track progress toward goals and make necessary adjustments.

Regular evaluation of financial strategies enables proactive decision-making, course correction, and optimization of resources to maximize returns and minimize risks. By maintaining a dynamic approach to financial management, we can remain agile and responsive to changing market dynamics and personal circumstances.

An integral part of strategic financial planning is cultivating a mindset of innovation and adaptability. Embracing innovation in financial practices, exploring new investment opportunities, and staying informed about emerging trends are strategic actions that can enhance financial growth and diversification. By remaining open to new possibilities and staying ahead of the curve, business owners can use innovation to drive financial success and capitalize on evolving market conditions.

Integrating strategic planning into financial endeavors is paramount to achieving long-term financial success, sustainability and prosperity. By adopting a strategic mindset, setting clear goals, conducting thorough research, implementing contingency measures, and fostering innovation, we can navigate the complex financial landscape with confidence and purpose.

As we adapt to market changes, our perceptions change and we gain the ability to predict future outcomes, which helps us minimize risk and even prepare for the worst. In fact, perception plays a central role in shaping the value and importance of money in our lives, while also expanding our ability to think beyond our current setbacks and challenges. But one of the biggest mistakes I see people make, and one that clearly describes their poverty mindset, is that they try to measure results in others by what they do.

People tend to think that the product defines a person's financial success and arrogantly assume a person's wealth potential based on their investments and beliefs, and they couldn't be more wrong, because it's not the product that defines results, it's the strategy. Those with a low sense of value see no strategy in anything because they confuse results with products. That is why they fail at everything they do, because the way they think about every idea is wrong from the start.

Understanding how perception shapes the concept of money provides insight into the complexities of human psychology, social dynamics, and economic systems. The poorer the understanding of money dynamics in a society, the more likely that society is to move toward its collective demise. In addition, the perception of money as a tangible representation of value is deeply rooted in our cultural and social norms, while also being a perfect mirror of a nation's economic situation. If citizens have a poor understanding of money, it will manifest itself in their own outcomes and at the national level.

Understanding the role of perception in shaping our attitudes toward money allows us to examine mindsets, beliefs, and biases about wealth and abundance, and also influences how we interact with money in our daily lives and social structures. Perceptions of money as a tool for empowerment, freedom, and opportunity can drive individuals to pursue entrepreneurial ventures, investment opportunities, and financial independence. On the other hand, negative perceptions of money as a source of stress, greed, or corruption can hinder financial growth and well-being.

Taken together, societal perceptions of money contribute to the construction of economic systems, financial institutions, and patterns of wealth distribution. The societal value placed on money shapes economic policies, social inequalities, and power dynamics within communities. Understanding the impact of societal perceptions on financial structures is critical to addressing systemic issues such as income inequality, poverty, and financial exclusion.

In sum, the interplay between money and perception underscores the complex relationship between individual beliefs, societal constructs, and economic realities. By acknowledging the influence of perception on the value and meaning of money, we can cultivate a positive mindset toward wealth, empower ourselves to pursue financial goals, and contribute to the creation of a more equitable and prosperous society. Adopting a mindset that values money as a tool for growth, impact, and well-being can lead to holistic transformation on both a personal and societal level.

Chapter 15: Sustainable Prosperity Through Wealth Management

Cultivating an abundance mindset is essential to reprogramming your relationship with money. Embracing the concept of abundance and wealth as a birthright can be a powerful catalyst for change. It involves shifting your focus from a mindset of scarcity to one of abundance, from fear to trust in the infinite possibilities of the universe. Visualizing a life of financial freedom, where money flows effortlessly and opportunities abound, can help align thoughts and actions to achieve these goals.

Meanwhile, cultivating a mindset of gratitude for the abundance already present in one's life can also help shift the focus from what is lacking to what is abundant. Practicing generosity by sharing wealth with others and contributing to causes that resonate with personal values not only enriches the lives of others, but also opens channels for receiving even more abundance in return.

By embracing financial freedom as a holistic journey of empowerment, you can transcend limitations, unlock your full potential, and create a life of abundance and prosperity that aligns with your deepest desires and aspirations. This abundance mindset also helps you cultivate resilience, which is essential for overcoming obstacles, adapting to unforeseen challenges and sustaining long-term success.

To develop strength in the face of adversity, there are certain principles and practices that can guide you. First, building a strong financial foundation is paramount. This includes practicing prudent budgeting, developing healthy savings habits, and making strategic investment choices. A strong foundation provides a safety net against unexpected financial shocks, allowing you to weather storms with greater ease.

It is also important to embrace risk and innovation in your financial endeavors. Taking calculated risks and exploring innovative strategies can lead to growth and success. Stepping out of your comfort zone, being open to new opportunities, and adapting to market changes are essential to thriving in a dynamic financial landscape.You also need to develop skills to effectively manage stress, uncertainty, and setbacks, as these will enhance your ability to make sound decisions under pressure. Learning to regulate emotions and communicate effectively can increase your resilience in challenging financial situations.

It is easier to cultivate such skills when you are informed about market trends, embrace new technologies, and explore innovative financial strategies that can help you adapt to changing circumstances and take advantage of new opportunities for growth, which is why you need to surround yourself with mentors, advisors, and peers who can provide guidance, perspective, and encouragement during challenging times. Cultivating relationships based on trust, collaboration, and mutual empowerment builds financial resilience and resourcefulness.

Flexibility and adaptability are key characteristics of financially resilient individuals, allowing them to easily adjust financial strategies and goals in response to changing circumstances. This adaptability is critical because it enables you to create a lasting legacy that spans generations. Sustainable wealth management is rooted in a set of fundamental principles and actions that provide the foundation for ensuring the seamless transfer of wealth over time.At the core of sustainable wealth management is strategic asset allocation, a cornerstone principle that involves creating a carefully tailored plan that aligns with your financial goals, risk tolerance and time horizon. By intelligently diversifying investments across a range of asset classes, you can effectively mitigate risk while optimizing returns over the long term, building a strong financial foundation for the future.

Complementing strategic asset allocation is the core element of long-term financial planning, an indispensable component of holistic wealth management strategies. By carefully creating a comprehensive financial roadmap that includes retirement planning, estate structuring, tax optimization and wealth preservation tactics, you can pave the way for a secure financial future and ensure the creation of a lasting legacy for generations to come.In the area of sustainable wealth management, the integration of impact investing and social responsibility is emerging as a driving force, reshaping investment paradigms with an ethos of conscious capitalism. Embracing these principles not only aligns investments with personal values, but also supports initiatives that promote environmental sustainability, foster positive social change, and generate impactful financial returns, embodying a harmonious blend of profit and purpose.Equally critical to sustainable wealth management is the facet of risk management and contingency planning, which serves as a bulwark against unforeseen adversities that could threaten financial stability. By proactively implementing robust risk mitigation strategies and contingency plans to address market fluctuations, economic uncertainties, or personal crises, you can protect your wealth and maintain lasting financial stability in the face of challenges.The application of proper, sustainable wealth management enables intergenerational wealth transfer, heralding a strategic approach to ensuring seamless continuity of assets and values across family lines. Using tools such as trusts, wills and family governance frameworks, you can orchestrate the transfer of wealth with precision and foresight, fostering a legacy of responsible stewardship and intergenerational prosperity. And by equipping future generations with the knowledge and skills necessary to navigate the complexities of financial decision-making, you can sow the seeds of lasting financial acumen and resilience for others, perpetuating a legacy of informed stewardship and sustainable prosperity.

Chapter 16: Societal Values and Individual Success in the Global Economy

The value placed on money varies across societies, encompassing traditional beliefs, modern trends, and evolving economic dynamics that shape perceptions of wealth and financial success and influence the distribution of wealth, access to opportunity, and economic mobility within a community. You may have more opportunities in one country than another, not necessarily because one nation is richer than another, but because your skills, ideas, and talents are valued and paid more in one place than another.

Many artists would find success if they knew how to seek it rather than force it. The same goes for writers who insist on a particular language instead of considering a variety of cultural and linguistic options. In business, too, you are more likely to succeed at what you do if you choose the right environment for it.

For example, one of the richest bakers I ever met was just average in France, but made his entire fortune very quickly in Shanghai, and he did not even have to change anything, he just had to keep doing what he was doing, which was making croissants, bread, and other pastries. He was not even a smart entrepreneur, but he was in the right place to manifest his dreams, and he even married a local woman.

Social value systems dictate the allocation of resources, the recognition of individual contributions, and the prioritization of economic activities that are consistent with collective values and goals. On the other hand, inequalities in wealth distribution often reflect underlying social hierarchies, power structures, and historical legacies that affect economic outcomes and social cohesion.

Your value as an individual is determined not by the perceptions of others, but by your location. Whatever your talent is, and whatever dream you wish to manifest, there is surely a place for it, or the dream would not come to you, and you would not have the talent to manifest it.

That's why I tell my followers not to worry about the unknown, because you don't have to know where or when your talent will manifest before you work on it. As you evolve toward the ideal dream in your mind, things will manifest for you. The land, the city, and the people will come to you.

This doesn't mean that you should stay in the land you find forever, but simply that there is a right place for everything, for every lesson, and for every necessary change. It is also true that you don't fail so much in what you do as you fail through the people you meet along the way.

Spending time with the right people can be critical to achieving your goals in life. But finding them isn't as important as learning what kind of people to say no to. Before you find the right people, you must learn to be alone and to say no to the many wrong people who come your way.

Likewise, before you find your path in life, you must fail and endure the frustration of going down the wrong paths. The value systems within a society shape individual aspirations, motivations, and attitudes toward money, influencing personal financial management, career choices, and lifestyle preferences that reflect societal norms and expectations, as well as how individuals within such societies perceive others and themselves.

Examining societal value systems related to money reveals the complex interplay between culture, economics, and human behavior, allowing you to properly assess your potential within this dynamic. Understanding how societal values influence the concept of money sheds light on the complexities of wealth distribution, economic development, and social cohesion within communities. You may not make friends in societies that don't share your values, while you may never feel alone in those that do.

This is why, while I struggled to have a normal conversation with the many idiots I found in Europe, including the many North American nomads I met there, I find it easy to make friends in Asian countries. Wisdom is simply not something that belongs to the West, but to the East. Accepting this reality has made it easier for me to improve my life, my well-being, write more books, achieve more financial success, and even find my soul mate.

You don't have to apologize for your life choices unless you feel you owe your future to your past and the people you found there. Often, accepting the reality in front of you and its negativity is the first step to recognizing the need to change location and find success elsewhere.

Chapter 17: Wealth Creation and Entrepreneurship in the Digital Age

The development of mobile payment systems and e-wallets has transformed the way people conduct everyday transactions, from purchasing goods and services to transferring funds and managing personal finances from anywhere in the world, making it very easy and accessible for anyone to move from one place to another on the planet. Today we can call such individuals nomads, but only because the masses haven't learned to normalize this dynamic and remain stuck in the previous societal stages, namely agrarian and industrial.

We have entered the post-industrial stage of society, which began to emerge in the late 20th century and continues to evolve today. But while today's society is often referred to as a post-industrial society because of the shift from manufacturing-based economies to service-based economies, the increasing role of technology and information in daily life is leading us into an entirely new stage.

This new social stage is characterized by mobile payment apps, contactless payment options and digital wallets, all of which have streamlined the transaction process, allowing users to pay conveniently from their smartphones, tablets or wearable devices. The convenience, speed and accessibility of mobile transactions have reshaped consumer behavior and merchant practices in the digital age, extending beyond digital currencies and mobile payments into the realm of e-commerce, online marketplaces and virtual assets.

These capabilities have made it easier to shop online, which in turn has facilitated the emergence of online businesses and opened a limitless horizon when it comes to the need to develop applications related to marketing and product management. Today, any teenager with access to the Internet can start an online business and sell virtually anything from anywhere in the world. The methods available are numerous and have been made so simple that anyone can become rich using only a computer or smartphone.

The proliferation of online shopping platforms, digital marketplaces, and virtual goods has blurred the lines between physical and digital transactions, creating new avenues for economic participation, value exchange, and wealth creation. Anyone can be an entrepreneur today, with nothing more than the will to do so. There are so many opportunities, you don't even need an idea anymore. There are many products that can be sold under any brand, and the brand is nothing more than a word.

The future of our economic systems lies in the convergence of technological innovations, regulatory frameworks, and consumer preferences that shape the landscape of financial interactions. But cultural attitudes toward money also influence spending habits, savings practices, and investment decisions around the world. Some cultures prioritize collective well-being and community support over individual wealth accumulation, while others emphasize personal financial success and material possessions as markers of achievement and happiness.

Exploring global perspectives on money reveals a tapestry of values, beliefs, and practices that underpin financial behaviors and economic interactions across diverse cultural landscapes. By exploring the multifaceted nature of money in a global context, we can gain deeper insight into the interconnectedness of economies, cultures, and human experiences in an increasingly interconnected world.

Money plays a significant role in contributing to personal fulfillment and satisfaction, intersecting with various aspects of human experience and well-being, but the relationship between money and fulfillment encompasses not only material abundance, but also spiritual, emotional, and relational considerations that shape an individual's sense of satisfaction and overall quality of life.

The pursuit of personal fulfillment through money often reflects deeper desires for security, freedom, and self-actualization. Money is seen as a means to meet basic needs, provide comfort, and create opportunities for growth and self-expression. But is it wrong to seek a life of abundance in order to enhance our self-esteem?

It all depends on how long you can endure feeling lost when society insists that money determines the value of your strategies and plans for the future. For example, for many years I was called crazy by people who did not believe I could succeed as a writer. This attitude toward my results persists today because many people don't believe I would do what I already do for a living.

Most people will not believe your ideas before you are successful, and may not believe them after you are successful, choosing instead to label you a criminal and a liar. Although many people seek financial stability and abundance as a way to achieve their goals, pursue their passions and experience a sense of accomplishment and satisfaction in life, this can come after many years of struggle, disappointment and frustration, so you won't experience happiness until you are comfortable with unhappiness. You don't experience wealth until you become comfortable with poverty. Some of the most successful entrepreneurs I know endured years of extreme poverty and hunger.

Chapter 18: Cultivating a Positive Relationship with Money

Cultivating a positive relationship with money involves aligning financial goals with personal values, ethical considerations, and a broader sense of purpose and meaning in life. Those who view money as a tool to enhance their well-being, contribute to the greater good, and support their life's purpose tend to experience a deeper sense of fulfillment and satisfaction.

The impact of money on personal fulfillment is intertwined with emotional well-being, mental health, and relationship dynamics. Financial challenges, debt, and scarcity can lead to stress, anxiety, and feelings of inadequacy that undermine an individual's sense of fulfillment and inner peace. On the other hand, financial security, abundance, and wise money management practices can foster a sense of confidence, empowerment, and emotional balance, increasing overall life satisfaction and well-being.

The pursuit of fulfillment through money also involves balancing material desires with spiritual growth, community involvement, and contributions to society. Individuals who view money as a tool for creating positive change, supporting meaningful causes, and nurturing relationships tend to experience a deeper sense of fulfillment and purpose in their financial pursuits. Finding harmony between financial success and holistic well-being involves integrating financial goals with personal growth, social responsibility, and spiritual principles to create a meaningful and fulfilling life.

Exploring money and its relationship to personal fulfillment reveals the multidimensional nature of wealth and well-being. By recognizing money as a resource for meeting both material and non-material needs, we can cultivate a balanced approach to financial management that aligns our financial goals with our values, aspirations, and overall vision for a fulfilling life. Money, when used thoughtfully and purposefully, has the potential to enhance personal fulfillment, promote happiness, and contribute to a life of meaning, joy, and satisfaction.

Cultivating a wealth mindset involves aligning one's emotions, beliefs, attitudes, and behaviors with the principles of abundance, success, and wealth creation in order to manifest desired financial outcomes. When we believe that our efforts are for the greater good, we are more likely to feel fulfilled, happy, and committed to wealth creation.

Rather than focusing solely on personal gain, individuals with a wealth mindset prioritize creating value for others through products or services that address specific needs and desires. By understanding market dynamics, identifying opportunities, and delivering exceptional value, we can reap financial rewards and build sustainable wealth over time.

At the same time, the importance of self-belief, self-confidence and positive self-talk in fostering a wealth mindset cannot be underestimated. A strong belief in one's abilities, worthiness for financial success, and ability to achieve one's goals is a powerful driver of wealth creation. Confidence empowers individuals to take calculated risks, seize opportunities, and persevere in the face of challenges.Positive self-talk also plays a critical role in shaping one's mindset toward abundance. By replacing negative thoughts and limiting beliefs with affirmations of success, abundance and prosperity, we can reprogram the subconscious mind to support our financial goals. This mindset shift can have a profound impact on behaviors, attitudes and actions, ultimately leading us to financial success.Maintaining a wealth mindset is about more than accumulating money. It is about adopting a set of beliefs, attitudes and behaviors that are consistent with the principles of abundance, success and prosperity. By cultivating a mindset rooted in value creation, discipline, responsibility, self-belief and confidence, we can position ourselves for financial abundance, fulfillment and long-term wealth creation.

Chapter 19: The Interplay of Financial Wellness and Mental Health

The deep connection between financial well-being and mental health cannot be overlooked. We must take a comprehensive approach to financial wellness that includes psychological resilience, emotional well-being and mental health awareness. The burden of financial challenges, debt and economic uncertainty can contribute significantly to feelings of anxiety, depression and emotional distress, which then affect our productivity and ability to make effective decisions.

It is wise to consider the need for mental health support and counseling services when facing financial stress or emotional challenges. Many of my successful followers sought my coaching services when they were feeling their worst and had no perspective on what to do with their lives, years before they found success. Consulting with mental health professionals, life coaches, therapists, or counselors can help you develop coping strategies, resilience skills, and emotional well-being practices that support your financial journey.

You are responsible for your actions and for seeking help from those who can help you, but learning from others about overcoming emotional difficulties can give you the resilience and self-awareness to make better financial decisions and manage relationship dynamics effectively.

You should also engage in self-care practices and stress reduction techniques by prioritizing activities that promote relaxation, mindfulness, physical health, and emotional balance. Some of these activities may include engaging with supportive communities, peer networks, or mental health advocacy groups. By connecting with others who understand your experience, you can cultivate empathy, shared understanding, and mutual support that contribute to mental health awareness and financial resilience. The combination of these strategies will empower you to face financial challenges with resilience, compassion, and mental clarity.

As we develop a higher wisdom about money, we understand the transformative power of mastering our emotions around money. Rather than forcing ourselves down paths that deny our individuality, we seek a self-therapeutic approach to reprogramming our beliefs and attitudes about wealth. This approach to life and money emphasizes ethical considerations in financial matters and illuminates the inextricable link between financial success, spiritual maturity, and psychological well-being.

In pursuing a life of financial abundance, we are called to align our financial aspirations with our deepest personal values and to cultivate an abundance mindset that goes beyond the mere accumulation of wealth. As we delve deeper into the intricate relationship between money and emotions, we come to understand how our emotional states affect our wealth, happiness, and spiritual fulfillment. We unravel the impact of our beliefs, subconscious mindset, and behavioral biases on our financial decisions, challenging us to adopt a wealth mindset, make informed decisions, and prioritize long-term strategies over immediate gains.Ultimately, the path to financial empowerment and prosperity requires a holistic approach - one that encompasses ethical wealth management, sustainable wealth, and a harmonious relationship with money and success. It is a journey that leads us to a deeper understanding of our values and purpose, and empowers us to create a legacy that transcends mere material wealth.As we walk this path, let us remember that true abundance is not measured in numbers alone, but in the richness of our spirit, the depth of our compassion, and the legacy of integrity we leave behind. May we walk this path with grace, wisdom, and an unwavering commitment to creating a world where financial empowerment is synonymous with spiritual fulfillment and true prosperity.

Glossary

Abundance Mindset: A perspective that views resources, opportunities, and wealth as plentiful and accessible.

Alchemy of Money: The transformative process of understanding and utilizing money as a form of energy and a tool for personal growth.

Altruistic Wealth Creation: Generating wealth with the intention of benefiting society and contributing to the greater good.

Collective Values: Shared beliefs, attitudes, and priorities within a society that influence economic systems and individual financial behaviors.

Consciousness: The state of awareness and perception that shapes one's understanding of wealth, success, and personal fulfillment.

Digital Age Economics: The economic landscape shaped by technological advancements, including digital currencies and online marketplaces.

Emotional Currency: The emotional associations and responses individuals have towards money.

Ethical Wealth Management: Managing financial resources in alignment with moral principles and social responsibility.

Financial Alchemy: The process of transforming one's relationship with money through spiritual and psychological practices.

Financial Empowerment: Gaining knowledge, skills, and confidence to make informed financial decisions.

Financial Resilience: The ability to withstand and recover from financial setbacks and adapt to changing economic circumstances.

Financial Wellness: The state of overall well-being related to one's financial situation, encompassing material prosperity and mental/emotional health.

Global Economy: The interconnected system of economic activities and financial exchanges across different countries and cultures.

Gross National Happiness (GNH): An alternative economic model prioritizing citizens' well-being and happiness over traditional measures of economic growth.

Holistic Prosperity: A comprehensive approach to wealth integrating financial success with spiritual growth and overall life satisfaction.

Illusory Nature of Money: The concept that money is a symbolic representation of value rather than an inherent source of worth or happiness.

Law of Attraction: The belief that positive or negative thoughts and attitudes can influence one's life experiences and financial outcomes.

Manifestation: The process of bringing desires and goals into reality through focused intention, belief, and action.

Money as Energy: The perspective that views money as a form of energy that flows and circulates to create opportunities and facilitate growth.

Perception of Wealth: How individuals and societies view and interpret the concept of wealth, influencing attitudes and behaviors related to money.

Personal Value Alignment: Ensuring that one's financial goals and practices are in harmony with personal values and life purpose.

Positive Financial Affirmations: Statements used to reprogram subconscious beliefs about money and wealth.

Prosperity Consciousness: A state of mind that is open to and expectant of abundance and success in all areas of life.

Scarcity Mindset: A perspective that views resources, including money, as limited and hard to come by.

Social Responsibility in Wealth: The idea that individuals and businesses have a duty to use their wealth in ways that benefit society.

Spiritual Economics: The integration of spiritual principles and practices into financial decision-making and wealth creation strategies.

Subconscious Beliefs: Deeply held attitudes and perceptions about money and wealth that operate below the level of conscious awareness.

Sustainable Prosperity: A long-term approach to wealth creation balancing financial success with environmental stewardship and social responsibility.

Symbolic Dance of Money: The complex interplay between money, personal values, societal norms, and individual behaviors.

Trust and Wealth: The relationship between financial prosperity and the ability to trust oneself, others, and the process of wealth creation.

Value Creation: The process of generating worth through products, services, or ideas that address specific needs or desires in the market.

Wealth Consciousness: A state of mind aligned with abundance, prosperity, and the unlimited potential for wealth creation.

Wealth Mindset: A set of beliefs, attitudes, and behaviors that support the creation and maintenance of financial abundance.

Book Review Request

Dear reader,

Thank you for purchasing this book! I would love to know your opinion. Writing a book review helps in understanding the readers and also impacts other readers' purchasing decisions. Your opinion matters. Please write a book review!

Your kindness is greatly appreciated!

About the Author

Dan Desmarques is a renowned author with a remarkable track record in the literary world. With an impressive portfolio of 28 Amazon bestsellers, including eight #1 bestsellers, Dan is a respected figure in the industry. Drawing on his background as a college professor of academic and creative writing, as well as his experience as a seasoned business consultant, Dan brings a unique blend of expertise to his work. His profound insights and transformational content appeal to a wide audience, covering topics as diverse as personal growth, success, spirituality, and the deeper meaning of life. Through his writing, Dan empowers readers to break free from limitations, unlock their inner potential, and embark on a journey of self-discovery and transformation. In a competitive self-help market, Dan's exceptional talent and inspiring stories make him a standout author, motivating readers to engage with his books and embark on a path of personal growth and enlightenment.

Also Written by the Author

1. 66 Days to Change Your Life: 12 Steps to Effortlessly Remove Mental Blocks, Reprogram Your Brain and Become a Money Magnet

2. A New Way of Being: How to Rewire Your Brain and Take Control of Your Life

3. Abnormal: How to Train Yourself to Think Differently and Permanently Overcome Evil Thoughts

4. Alignment: The Process of Transmutation Within the Mechanics of Life

5. Audacity: How to Make Fast and Efficient Decisions in Any Situation

6. Christ Cult Codex: The Untold Secrets of the Abrahamic Religions and the Cult of Jesus

7. Codex Illuminatus: Quotes & Sayings of Dan

Desmarques

8. Collective Consciousness: How to Transcend Mass Consciousness and Become One With the Universe

9. Creativity: Everything You Always Wanted to Know About How to Use Your Imagination to Create Original Art That People Admire

10. Deception: When Everything You Know about God is Wrong

11. Demigod: What Happens When You Transcend The Human Nature?

12. Discernment: How Do Your Emotions Affect Moral Decision-Making?

13. Eclipsing Mediocrity: How to Unveil Hidden Realities and Master Life's Challenges

14. Fearless: Powerful Ways to Get Abundance Flowing into Your Life

15. Feel, Think and Grow Rich: 4 Elements to Attract Success in Life

16. Find Your Flow: How to Get Wisdom and Knowledge from God

17. Holistic Psychology: 77 Secrets about the Mind That They Don't Want You to Know

18. How to Change the World: The Path of Global Ascension Through Consciousness
19. How to Get Lucky: How to Change Your Mind and Get Anything in Life
20. How to Improve Your Self-Esteem: 34 Essential Life Lessons Everyone Should Learn to Find Genuine Happiness
21. How to Study and Understand Anything: Discovering The Secrets of the Greatest Geniuses in History
22. Legacy: How to Build a Life Worth Remembering
23. Religious Leadership: The 8 Rules Behind Successful Congregations
24. Reset: How to Observe Life Through the Hidden Dimensions of Reality and Change Your Destiny
25. Resilience: The Art of Confronting Reality Against the Odds
26. Singularity: What to Do When You Lose Hope in Everything
27. Spiritual Warfare: What You Need to Know About Overcoming Adversity
28. Starseed: Secret Teachings about Heaven and the Future of Humanity

29. Technocracy: The New World Order of the Illuminati and The Battle Between Good and Evil

30. The 10 Laws of Transmutation: The Multidimensional Power of Your Subconscious Mind

31. The 14 Karmic Laws of Love: How to Develop a Healthy and Conscious Relationship With Your Soulmate

32. The 33 Laws of Persistence: How to Overcome Obstacles and Upgrade Your Mindset for Success

33. The 36 Laws of Happiness: How to Solve Urgent Problems and Create a Better Future

34. The Alchemy of Truth: Embracing Change and Transcending Time

35. The Antagonists: What Makes a Successful Person Different?

36. The Antichrist: The Grand Plan of Total Global Enslavement

37. The Awakening: How to Turn Darkness Into Light and Ascend to Higher Dimensions of Existence

38. The Egyptian Mysteries: Essential Hermetic Teachings for a Complete Spiritual Reformation

39. The Evil Within: The Spiritual Battle in Your Mind Deception: When Everything You Know about God is

Wrong

40. The Game of Life and How to Play It: How to Get Anything You Want in Life

41. The Hidden Language of God: How to Find a Balance Between Freedom and Responsibility

42. The Most Powerful Quotes: 400 Motivational Quotes and Sayings

43. The Secret Beliefs of The Illuminati: The Complete Truth About Manifesting Money Using The Law of Attraction That is Being Hidden From You

44. The Secret Empire: The Hidden Truth Behind the Power Elite and the Knights of the New World Order

45. The Secret Science of the Soul: How to Transcend Common Sense and Get What You Really Want From Life

46. The Spiritual Laws of Money: The 31 Best-kept Secrets to Life-long Abundance

47. The Spiritual Mechanics of Love: Secrets They Don't Want You to Know about Understanding and Processing Emotions

48. Unacknowledged: How Negative Emotions Affect Your Mental Health?

49. Unapologetic: Taking Control of Your Mind for a Happier and Healthier Life
50. Uncommon: Transcending the Lies of the Mental Health Industry
51. Unlocked: How to Get Answers from Your Subconscious Mind and Control Your Life
52. Your Full Potential: How to Overcome Fear and Solve Any Problem
53. Your Soul Purpose: Reincarnation and the Spectrum of Consciousness in Human Evolution

About the Publisher

This book was published by 22 Lions Publishing.

www.22Lions.com